GO TO CLASS: HOW TO SUCCEED AT COLLEGE

KAREN DENTLER

Published by Goose Pond Productions

Cover Art and Interior by Ashley Ruggirello

Learn about bulk ordering and speaking engagements at collegegiftbook.com or @collegegiftbook.

Hardcover ISBN: 979-8-9869515-7-7

Paperback ISBN: 979-8-9869515-2-2

IN TRO DUC TION

Go to class.

It seems obvious; it seems simple. Nevertheless, I have had to give that advice to many students over my long career in higher education. Students would arrive in my office upset, stressed, crying, scared, withdrawn, or confused. Once they started talking, students would frantically explain that they were failing a class (or often, just not currently getting their typical A). I would let them vent and then simply ask: "Are you going to class?"

No, they would admit. The professor is unfair. The course is too hard. I've been sick. I've been busy with other "more important" classes. The professor doesn't take attendance. The class is too early.

If you can think of an excuse, I have heard it.

As part of our conversation, we would review graduation requirements and develop an academic plan. I referred students to campus resources, such as the learning or counseling centers. We would discuss strategies for success. Yet before they left my office, I always got a commitment that they would start going to class. We would agree that they would attend class for an entire week, and then come back for another appointment to check in on their progress. When students came back, they often felt much better. To put it in philosophical terms, going to class is necessary, but not always sufficient for success at college.

Therefore, the title of this book — and the first tip — is "Go to class." In this book, I've tried to distill all of the advice that I've been giving to students for 20 years. Comprehensive personalized advising is not always available to students, and even when good advising is readily available, students may not always take advantage of it. Yet good advice is essential to success at college. With this book, I want to help all students succeed and make the most of their college education.

I did not leave college until I was 48. I went to my first school, Colgate University, in 1987 and left my last school, Rutgers, The State University of New Jersey, in 2017. At Rutgers, I spent 10 years as an Assistant Dean for the School of Arts and Sciences Honors Program. Some of the advice in this book originates from my interactions with this amazing group of students. I advised over 400 students each year, watching them adapt to college, struggle, succeed, and launch into careers, graduate programs, and post-graduate fellowships. Throughout my career, I have been a student, graduate student, teacher, academic adviser, student affairs professional, and policymaker, working and studying at rural, suburban, and urban colleges and universities, including small private schools, large public research universities, and an Ivy League institution.

I am also the mother of a college student. Throughout my daughter's college search, I had the opportunity to see the admissions process from the other side. After my experiences speaking at countless recruitment events, reading hundreds of essays, and reviewing numerous transcripts, now the shoe was on the other foot. As my conversations with other parents inevitably turned to college, I realized that my perspective was unique. I saw and heard things during campus visits that other parents and kids didn't notice. As a parent with a background in higher education, I know that it isn't just what the admission representatives say, but how they say it, and which statistics and programs they choose to highlight. On the campus tour, it isn't just what the student tour guide showcases, but also what the tour leaves out. Of course, each school puts its best foot forward, but I see the nuances between each school's approaches to education and student life. My hope is that my career has prepared me to help my most important advisee, my daughter. Before she left for college, I gave her a copy of this book.

-K.D.

CHAPTER ONE

LEARN

CLASSES, REGISTRATION, AND GPA

GO

TO

CLASS.

Go to class, even if the professor doesn't take attendance. **Be on time,** even when the class is early in the morning. Going to class doesn't solve every academic problem, but it is hard to resolve any issue without completing this essential first step.

CHOOSE A SEAT AT THE *FRONT* OF THE CLASSROOM.

This simple act makes the room, even if it's a large lecture hall, feel more intimate. A front seat will motivate you to fully engage with the material.

Participate in class.

Share your ideas and ask questions.

If you are going to miss a class,

REPORT YOUR ABSENCE

to the professor in advance.

Most professors have their **attendance policies and procedures** on the class **syllabus.** Professors truly appreciate when you let them know that you will be absent from class. **Talk with the professor** in person or via email as soon as possible about your plans to make up missed work and hand in assignments.

By the way...

- [ ] **DO**
- [ ] **READ**
- [ ] **THE**
- [ ] **SYLLABUS.**

Each academic discipline has its own style of writing.

Writing up a lab report requires different skills than writing a history paper. Learn to adapt your writing to each subject.

and

grammar & spelling matter

DON'T PLAGIARIZE OR CHEAT.

Be sure that you fully understand your school's academic integrity standards. Academic dishonesty — even if it's unintentional — can result in a failing grade, suspension, or expulsion.

All courses that bear **credit** are **useful.** They count in your credit total, broaden your education, and bring you closer to your degree.

If you want to learn about something cool, **do it now.** Take a few classes solely because they sound **interesting.** After college, it is likely that all of your learning will be focused on a particular skill or career.

Register for your next semester's classes as soon as you are **eligible,** even if you have a cold, even if you have a paper to write, even if you are at a meeting. Registering **late** almost always means a big **headache.**

CREATE MULTIPLE VERSIONS OF ACCEPTABLE SCHEDULES.

Understand the **deadlines** and **procedures** for **dropping** and **adding** classes at the start of the semester.

FIND OUT THE PROCESS AT YOUR SCHOOL FOR GETTING INTO A CLOSED CLASS. "CLOSED" DOESN'T ALWAYS MEAN CLOSED.

UNDERSTAND THAT YOUR GPA MAY

FLUCTUATE

especially during your first few semesters. Remember how an average works. As you accumulate more credits in your total, each individual grade impacts the GPA less and less.

CHAPTER TWO
PLAN

REQUIREMENTS, MAJORS, RESEARCH, AND CAREERS

Meet with an academic **adviser** at least **once** per semester. Think of meeting with your adviser as a medical checkup. You should not wait until you are really sick to get treatment.

Talking about your academic plans with an adviser helps you **connect** with the **right resources** at the right time.

The best academic plans are flexible and provide

MULTIPLE PATHS TO GRADUATION.

Plan just one semester of specific courses at a time. If it helps you sleep at night, feel free to plan out all four years, but keep in mind that your first-year plan may not end up being your final plan.

Reviewing your graduation requirements often is the best way to **avoid surprises** and the dreaded "you are not going to graduate" email in the spring of your senior year.

A complete **understanding** of your **requirements** makes choosing your classes each semester **less stressful.**

Go to your professors' **office hours** just to chat or ask them about their work. Professors appreciate when students **take an interest** in their research.

This will help you develop a **personal connection** with your professors that may lead to future conversations where they can provide **meaningful advice** about their discipline, college, careers, graduate school, and life in general.

Get involved with research at your university.

Research is the lifeblood of higher education.

Remember that **all departments do research,** not just the sciences. For example, economists might have students collect and analyze data. English departments may conduct archival research or compile poetry databases, and molecular biology professors could bring several students into their labs to assist with experiments on cell membrane molecules.

Being a part of a research project or working in a lab will **enhance your understanding** of concepts in the classroom and expand your knowledge of the world, along with providing valuable **hands-on experience.**

Research projects can provide you with academic **credit,** networking opportunities, and a chance to **publish** your results or **present** them at a professional conference.

To find a research **opportunity,** **talk** with your current professors and the adviser from your major department on how to **get started.**

Many majors prepare you for multiple career paths.

JUST BECAUSE A MINOR OR CERTIFICATE EXISTS, IT DOESN'T NECESSARILY MEAN THAT YOU NEED TO COMPLETE IT.

Taking one or two extra classes that you won't find interesting to get a piece of paper is a waste of time. Most employers simply want to know what you learned, the strength of your interpersonal skills, and what you can accomplish for their organization.

If possible, **explore** a few options **before** selecting your **major.**

Consider departments where you've succeeded in a few courses and find the discipline **interesting.**

DON'T CHOOSE YOUR MAJOR BECAUSE YOU WANTED THAT CAREER WHEN YOU WERE FIVE AND CAN'T THINK OF ANYTHING ELSE TO DO.

Make your **own** academic choices. Don't plan your schedule around your best friends. Don't plan your schedule around your family's ambitions. It is **your education.**

If you genuinely want a specific major or career, don't let anything stand in your way. When embarking on a challenging professional path, strategize about how to approach the long road ahead. Develop strategies for coping with stress and disappointment, but believe that you can reach your goal. Persist.

Go to **career services** at the beginning of your sophomore year. During your first year, it is best to acclimate to college and explore different disciplines. By sophomore year, it is time to start **thinking ahead.**

Aside from the obvious help with resumes and internships, career advisers usually have an **interesting** and **useful** perspective on selecting a major.

Do an internship.

GOOD INTERNSHIPS CAN LEAD TO JOB OFFERS. BAD INTERNSHIPS CAN HELP YOU LEARN WHAT YOU DON'T WANT TO DO.

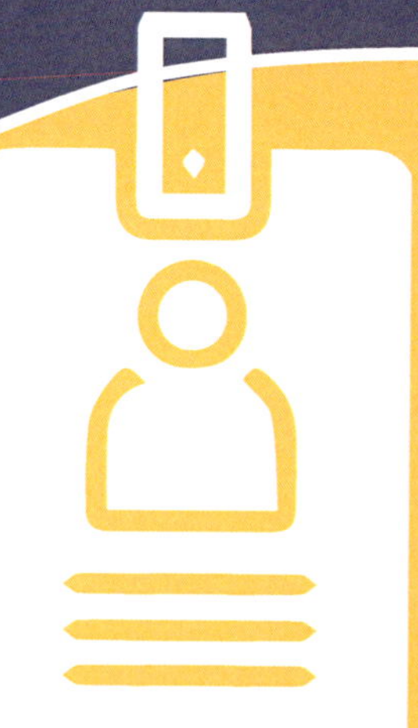

Before you apply to a **graduate program,** talk with people who have the degree and **be sure** you want or need it.

College is **short;** life is **long.** Just because it may be possible to graduate early, it doesn't always mean it is a good idea.

Graduating early can let you **save** money and **get started** on a career path or graduate school program. However, remaining in college for four years has **benefits:** serving as a resident assistant or student organization officer, giving you the time to write a thesis, completing a research project, or taking advantage of student-only internship opportunities.

CHAPTER THREE

ADAPT

HIDDEN RESOURCES, ACADEMIC POLICY, AND OVERCOMING OBSTACLES

Tutoring can be the difference between an A and B or a B and C. More importantly, tutoring is always the difference between being stressed or not stressed. If you are taking a difficult class, **go to tutoring** every week from the start of the semester. Even if you don't think you need it, go anyway.

Your school's **learning center** is not just for tutoring. Most centers can also **help you** improve your study habits, manage test anxiety, develop textbook-reading or note-taking strategies, strengthen time management, and combat procrastination.

Take advantage of your school's **writing center.** Writing centers help with all college writing assignments from English papers to lab reports, and they can provide **valuable and time-saving guidance** at the beginning, middle, or end of your writing process.

ASK FACULTY AND STAFF ABOUT *scholarship opportunities* **FOR CURRENT STUDENTS.**

Save money on **books** by researching your options, including rentals, used copies, and electronic subscriptions. Always **compare prices** and don't forget to find out which books are available for free at the library. **Get recommendations** from other students and your professors.

CHECK YOUR COLLEGE EMAIL EVERY DAY

during the semester.

Read your school email regularly during breaks and over the summer too. You do not want to miss important announcements about upcoming deadlines, policy changes, new courses, or special opportunities.

When emailing faculty and staff, **be professional.** Treat emails like business letters, not casual texts.

Be sure to include your full name and, when appropriate, your student ID number to **make yourself easily identifiable.**

If you need a letter of recommendation, give the person **at least 2-4 weeks** to write it. Offer to meet the reference in person and provide a resume.

Fill out all school forms and paperwork in advance.

Get any **exceptions or modifications** to your requirements in writing.

Staff retire. Professors forget. Policies change. **Get it in writing,** and make sure any exceptions are reflected in the school's system.

If you need **credits**, talk with an adviser about taking a class online or at your local community college **over the summer.**

Be sure to fully understand your school's policies, procedures, and deadlines for **transferring** credits. Do not just take a class and assume it will transfer.

KNOW YOUR SCHOOL'S REPEATED COURSE POLICY.

Only repeat a course if you really need that specific course to graduate. If there is another option to complete the same requirement, strongly consider it. Don't retake a course just because you are not happy with the grade. **Move on.**

If you get the dreaded "you are not going to graduate" email, take a deep breath and read it through **carefully.** If the problem is an administrative issue, such as unpaid parking tickets or a miscommunication between your major department and your school, **politely** respond to the email, then **get to work** to resolve it.

You may need to hand-deliver paperwork from one office to another or get up early to visit several offices. If you are truly missing a requirement, make an appointment to **talk with an adviser** to discuss your options and develop a plan to complete the outstanding requirement. Ask if you can still participate in the graduation ceremony.

If you oversleep during finals but your test is still in progress,

— DON'T WALK —

to the final. Your professor may still let you take it. If the final is over, email, call, and find your professor immediately to see about your options for possibly making it up. In the future, set multiple alarms.

If you know you are going to miss several classes due to an extended illness or emergency, **contact** your adviser or a dean of students. Your dean or adviser can help you approach all of your professors **at once** and help verify the legitimacy of an extended absence. Generally, the more people you bring into the loop to help you during a crisis, the better chance you will have to **successfully** complete your courses.

Withdrawing from a class is **not** going to ruin your life. A pattern of Ws, such as one every semester, might concern an employer or graduate school, but it is very common to have one or two W grades on a transcript. Every moment you spend on a class that you end up dropping is time that you could have been spending on classes that you are committed to completing.

Once you make your decision to stay or withdraw, **don't obsess;** just move on. Unless you take upper-level physics and build a time machine, you need to make the **best** possible decisions in real time and keep moving forward.

If you have an incomplete grade or outstanding work from a previous semester,

ALWAYS COMPLETE IT BEFORE EMBARKING ON NEW CLASSES.

It is never a good idea to start a new semester already behind.

IT IS **100% FINE** NOT TO GET AN A. YOUR LIFE IS NOT RUINED IF YOU GET A C, D, OR F. NO SINGLE GRADE REPRESENTS THE END OF YOUR EDUCATIONAL JOURNEY.

After a disappointing semester, do a bit of soul-searching and talk with a **trusted** adviser. Honestly examine what happened. Were your grades the result of a temporary issue that is now resolved? Do you need to change your study habits, academic plan, major, or next semester schedule? **Be realistic.**

Easy (GPA-booster) classes are fine, but use them **sparingly** and **strategically.** Light classes can help you regain your confidence after a disappointing semester or lighten your workload during a busy time.

If you need to take a leave of absence for personal or financial reasons, leave, and come back **later.** Don't stay and waste your time and money. Return only when you are **truly ready** to resume your education. While transitioning back to school, keep an open line of **communication** with your advisers and professors, and adhere to your school's withdrawal and re-enrollment deadlines.

When returning to school after a health issue, seek and follow the **advice** of medical and mental health professionals, and make sure you have a **support network** in place to help you.

You are paying for college; take advantage of your school's free resources.

CHAPTER FOUR

LIVE

STUDENT INVOLVEMENT, RESIDENCE LIFE, AND WELLNESS

DON'T FORGET TO
sleep.
STAYING UP ALL NIGHT
USUALLY PRODUCES
LOUSY PAPERS AND TEST
RESULTS.
ZZZ

EXERCISE.

USE THE GYM.

TAKE A FITNESS CLASS.

JOIN A RECREATIONAL LEAGUE.

TRY OUT FOR A TEAM.

If you or another student needs help or advice, **reach out** to someone, such as a counselor, RA, professor, dean, student life professional, or other university staff member.

Use the **counseling center.** It is free and confidential. (The world would be a better place if everyone had free counseling.)

If you are concerned about someone, but the person is **apprehensive** about calling the counseling center, **offer** to be in the room while your friend makes an appointment, or just travel to the counseling center together.

Be safe at parties. If someone needs medical help, **get help.** Do not let peer pressure or fear of getting in trouble prevent you from calling for help. Do not assume someone else will do it. You may save someone else's life.

Join clubs and student organizations. Take leadership roles in your favorite ones. These positions **enhance** your college experience, interpersonal skills, and resume.

Go to lots of campus **lectures** and **performances.** After college, you will no longer have constant access to **free** high-quality performances and thought-provoking lectures from famous (or soon to be famous) people.

Attend campus events with free food, but don't eat pizza every day.

Give back to the college community and the community surrounding your school. **Get involved** with community service.

Live on campus your first year, if possible. If you commute, join a student organization or find other ways to **get involved.** Getting connected to the school community greatly increases your chance of **success** at college.

Strongly consider **special interest housing.** Many schools have separate residence halls for specific communities or interests. Choosing to live in this type of housing often comes with significant **benefits** including exclusive events, mentors, advisers, and courses.

If you are having problems in your residence hall,

talk with your RA.

RAs generally receive comprehensive training and are skilled in assisting residents with a wide range of personal issues. Working closely with professional staff, RAs often resolve roommate conflicts, give advice, and refer students to campus resources. If talking with your RA doesn't help, talk with professional residence life staff or a dean of students.

VS

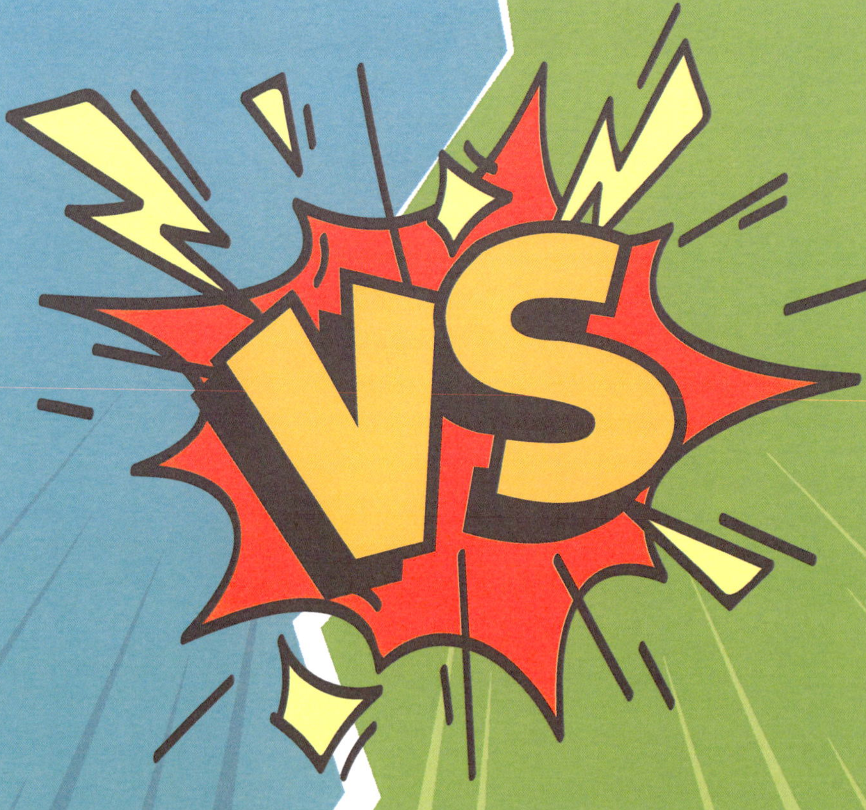

RAs try to cultivate a sense of community by hosting **special events and programs** in the residence halls. Attending RA-sponsored events is a perfect way to get to know your neighbors and develop new connections.

STAY IN TOUCH WITH YOUR FAMILY AND FRIENDS FROM HOME.
Connecting with your college community is essential to success, but keeping a strong support network from home is also important. Your friends and family miss you.

CHAPTER FIVE

KNOW

REFLECTIONS ON EDUCATION

Hone your writing, speaking, and visual presentation skills. Great ideas are useless if you can't explain them.

Learn to **communicate clearly** and organize your thoughts.

SEEK OUT OPPORTUNITIES TO PRACTICE PUBLIC SPEAKING, EVEN IF YOU DON'T ENJOY IT. LIFE AND WORK OFTEN REQUIRE SPEAKING TO GROUPS.

Study abroad, if possible. It will broaden your perspective on how to live, work, and, of course, study.

Learn to speak another language. Many organizations and graduate programs want people who are multilingual.

Learn about issues that matter to you.

Get involved.

Register and **vote** during college if you are an eligible voter. Elections happen every year and local and midterm elections matter. Your vote is your voice, and voting is **essential** to a functioning democracy. Consider volunteering for a campaign or running for office.

College is an environment where you can **connect** with people who have different views and experiences. Take the opportunity to get to know a diverse group of students.

DEBATE IMPORTANT IDEAS.

College is the time to exchange ideas with people who have different perspectives on topics like politics, public policy, and economics.

DEBATE DUMB IDEAS.

College is also about staying up all night arguing about the best place to get dumplings or what actually happens when a tree falls in the forest.

Your education should be about more than getting a job. It should also be about

learning how to live a good life.

Scientists need to know about politics. Business leaders need to understand humanities and history.

The boundaries between academic departments are arbitrary and in constant flux.

Recognize that true knowledge is interdisciplinary.

www.ingramcontent.com/pod-product-compliance
Ingram Content Group UK Ltd.
Pitfield, Milton Keynes, MK11 3LW, UK
UKRC032148290726
14090UKWH00012B/499